Nico Muhly

# THE RIGHT OF YOUR SENSES

for soprano solo, children's choir and orchestra

Study score

St Rose Music Publishing Co.
/ Chester Music Ltd.

Co-commissioned by the National Children's Chorus, American Youth Symphony & Los Angeles Philharmonic Association, Gustavo Dudamel, Music & Artistic Director. The first performance was given on 31 March 2019 at Walt Disney Concert Hall, Los Angeles, California, U.S.A.

## INSTRUMENTATION

Piccolo
2 Flutes
2 Oboes
Cor Anglais
2 Clarinets in B♭
Bass Clarinet
2 Bassoons
Contrabassoon

4 Horns in F
3 Trumpets in C
2 Trombones
Bass Trombone
Tuba

Timpani
Percussion (4 players):
    Crotales (with bow), Glockenspiel, Vibraphone (with bow),
    Egg Shaker, Large Maraca, High 'Piccolo' Wood Block,
    2 Triangles (very high and low),
    2 Tom-toms (tuned approximately a minor third apart), Brake Drum,
    2 Tam-tams (medium and large), Bass Drum

Harp
Piano

Soprano Solo
Children's Choir

Strings

Duration: c. 25 minutes

Full score in C.

Orchestral parts are available on hire from the publisher.

## COMPOSER'S NOTE

*The Right of Your Senses* is a set of nine songs for children's voices, solo soprano, and orchestra written for the National Children's Chorus, American Youth Symphony and Los Angeles Philharmonic Association. The texts are primarily 17th-century, by Thomas Traherne and George Herbert, but two of them come from the 11th-century *Enchiridion* by Byrhtferth. The overarching theme is the story of creation, but not just the list of objects created: the texts deal with the emotional resonances of the sun, the sea, the air, and the moon with all their mysterious, bright, and dark potential. There is a recurring gesture in the strings, introduced at the very top: a simple descending pattern which binds many of the movements together, even when hidden in the more tumultuous sections. The first two movements are bright, whereas the middle three movements are violent and deal with the angrier natural elements. The seventh movement is the most abstract and playful, and here a direct nod to Benjamin Britten's *A Ceremony of Carols*, with a fast three-part canon depicting the behavior of the atom. The eighth movement, *Night*, is the slowest, and depicts the night sky. The final movement is calm, and encourages us: "Be faithful in a little, and you shall be master over much." The piece ends with five strokes of high bells.

# TEXTS

## - 1 -

Is it not easy to conceive the World in your Mind? To think the Heavens fair? The Sun Glorious? The Earth fruitful? The Air Pleasant? The Sea Profitable? And the Giver bountiful? The entrance of His words giveth Light to the simple.

*Centuries of Meditation*
Thomas Traherne (1636–74)

## - 2 -

On the fourth day [...] he created the sun and moon and stars and all planets, and at dawn of that day the bright sun rose right at the eastern edge of heaven, and on the same evening he placed the moon in the same place, and it was as full as it is when it is fifteen days old.

*Enchiridion*
Byrhtferth (c.970–1020)

## - 3 -

The dividing of the sea, the commanding of the sun, the making of the world is nothing to the single creation of one soul. To love one person with a private love is poor and miserable: to love all is glorious. To love all persons in all ages, all angels, all worlds, is Divine and Heavenly. To love all cities and all kingdoms, all kings and all peasants, and every person in all worlds with a natural intimate familiar love, as if him alone, is Blessed.

*Centuries of Meditation*
Thomas Traherne

## - 4 -

Frost must freeze, fire burn up wood,
the earth grow, ice form bridges,
water wear a covering, wondrously locking up
shoots in the earth. One alone shall unbind
the frost's fetters: God most mighty.
Winter shall turn, good weather come again,
summer bright and hot. The never-resting sea,
the deep way of the dead, will be the longest hidden.

*The Menologium*
Anglo-Saxon (9th Century)

## - 5 -

If as the winds and waters here below
Do fly and flow,
My sighs and tears as busy were above;
Sure they would move
And much affect thee, as tempestuous times
Amaze poor mortals, and object their crimes.

Stars have their storms, ev'n in a high degree,
As well as we.
A throbbing conscience spurred by remorse
Hath a strange force:
It quits the earth, and mounting more and more,
Dares to assault, and besiege thy door.

There it stands knocking, to thy musick's wrong,
And drowns the song.
Glory and honour are set by till it
An answer get.
Poets have wrong'd poor storms: such days are best;
They purge the air without, within the breast.

*The Storm*
George Herbert (1593–1633)

## - 6 -

[June], in which the jewel climbs up
into the heavens highest in the year,
brightest of stars, and descends from its place,
sinks to its setting. It likes then to gaze longer

upon the earth, the fairest of lights
to move more slowly across the fields of the world,
the created globe.

The Menologium

## - 7 -

A long Atom is a Contradiction in Nature.
So is a round one, for that hath circumference.
A Triangle, a Square, a Hooked Atom is nonsense,
for in ev'ry Angle there will be an Atom truly.
A hook must of necessity have parts out of Parts, or else it cannot be crooked.

Centuries of Meditation<br>Thomas Traherne

## - 8 -

The stars have us to bed;
Night draws the curtain, which the sun withdraws;
Music and light attend our head.
All things unto our flesh are kind
In their descent and being; to our mind
In their ascent and cause.

Man<br>George Herbert

## - 9 -

By the very right of your senses you enjoy the world. Is not the beauty of the hemisphere present to your eye? Doth not the glory of the sun pay tribute to your sight? Is not the vision of the world an amiable thing? Do not the stars shed influences to perfect the air? Is not that a marvellous body to breathe in? To visit the lungs: repair the spirits: revive the senses: cool the blood: fill the empty spaces between the earth and heavens; and yet give liberty to all objects?

Be faithful in a little, and you shall be master over much.

Centuries of Meditation<br>Thomas Traherne

*for Luke McEndarfer & Jessica Rivera*

# THE RIGHT OF YOUR SENSES

Nico Muhly
(2019)

## 1. The World in Your Mind

*Centuries of Meditations*
Thomas Traherne

**Moving** ♩ = 108

| | |
|---|---|
| Piccolo | |
| Flute 1 | |
| Flute 2 | |
| Oboe 1.2 | |
| Cor Anglais | |
| Clarinet 1.2 in B♭ | |
| Bass Clarinet | |
| Bassoon 1.2 | |
| Contrabassoon | |
| Horn 1.2 in F | |
| Horn 3.4 in F | |
| Trumpet 1–3 in C | |
| Trombone 1.2 | |
| Bass Trombone | |
| Tuba | |
| Timpani | |
| Vibraphone (arco) | |
| Egg Shaker Large Maraca | |
| Harp | |
| Piano | |
| Soprano Solo | |
| Children's Choir | |
| Violin I | |
| Violin II | |
| Viola | |
| Cello | |
| Double Bass | |

Children's Choir text: Is it not ea-sy to con-ceive the World in your Mind? To think the

Piano: plucked inside piano

Violin II: back 2 stands only

Viola: bell-like

Double Bass: pizz. div.

**Moving** ♩ = 108

Hea - vens   fair?        The   Sun_____ Glo - ri - ous?        The   Earth_____ fruit - ful?        The

# 2. At the Dawn of that Day

73
Picc.
Fl. 1.2
Ob. 1.2
C. A.
Cl. 1.2
B. Cl.
sempre staccatiss.
Bsn. 1
Bsn. 2
Cbsn.
Hn. 1.2
Hn. 3.4
Tpt. 1
Tpt. 2
Tpt. 3
Tbn. 1.2
B. Tbn.
Tba.
Timp.
Crot.
Vib.
W.B.
B. D.
Hp.
Pno.
Vln. I
all notes ♪
Vln. II
all notes ♪
div.
Vla.
molto
Vc.
Db.

# 3. The Sea

*Centuries of Meditations*
Thomas Traherne

22

and ev-'ry per-son in all worlds_____ with a na-tu-ral____ in-ti-mate fa-mi-liar love____

24

S. Solo: To love all\_\_\_\_\_ per - sons,\_\_\_\_\_

Ch.: as if him a - lone,\_\_\_\_\_ is Bless - ed. To love all\_\_\_\_\_ per - sons, in all\_\_\_\_\_

# 4. Frost

*The Menologium (or Maxims I?)*
Anglo-Saxon

29

# 5. Storm

*The Storm*
George Herbert

If as the winds and wa-ters here_____ be- low     Do fly_____ and flow._____

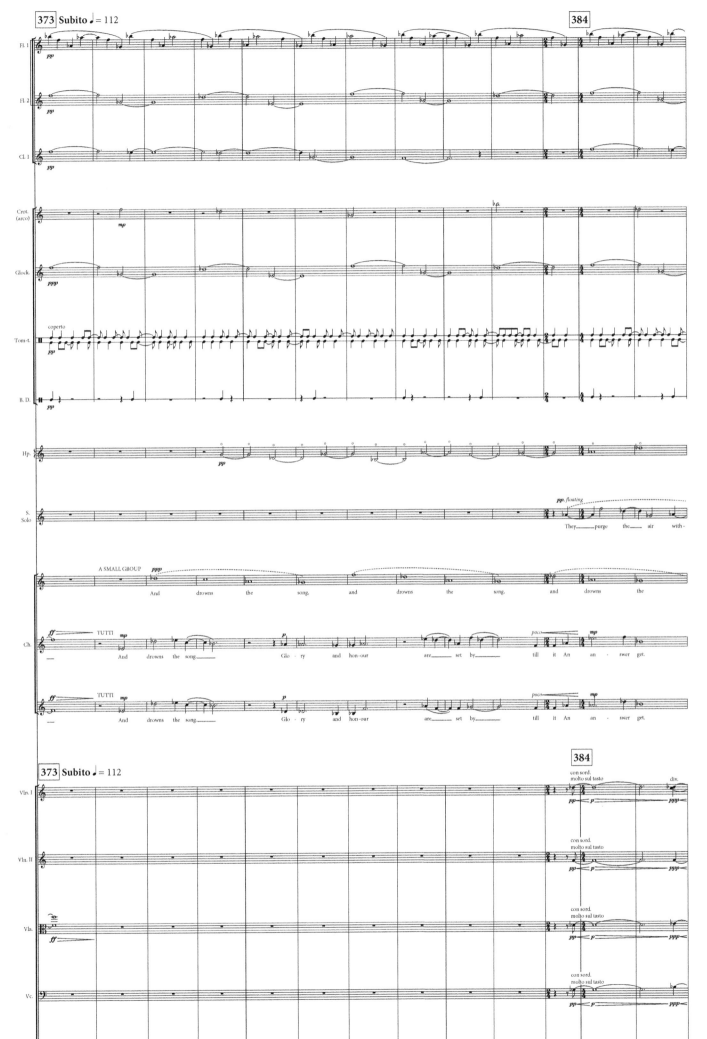

# 6. The Fairest of Lights

*The Menologium*
Anglo-Saxon

# 7. An Atom

*Centuries of Meditations*
Thomas Traherne

501

attacca

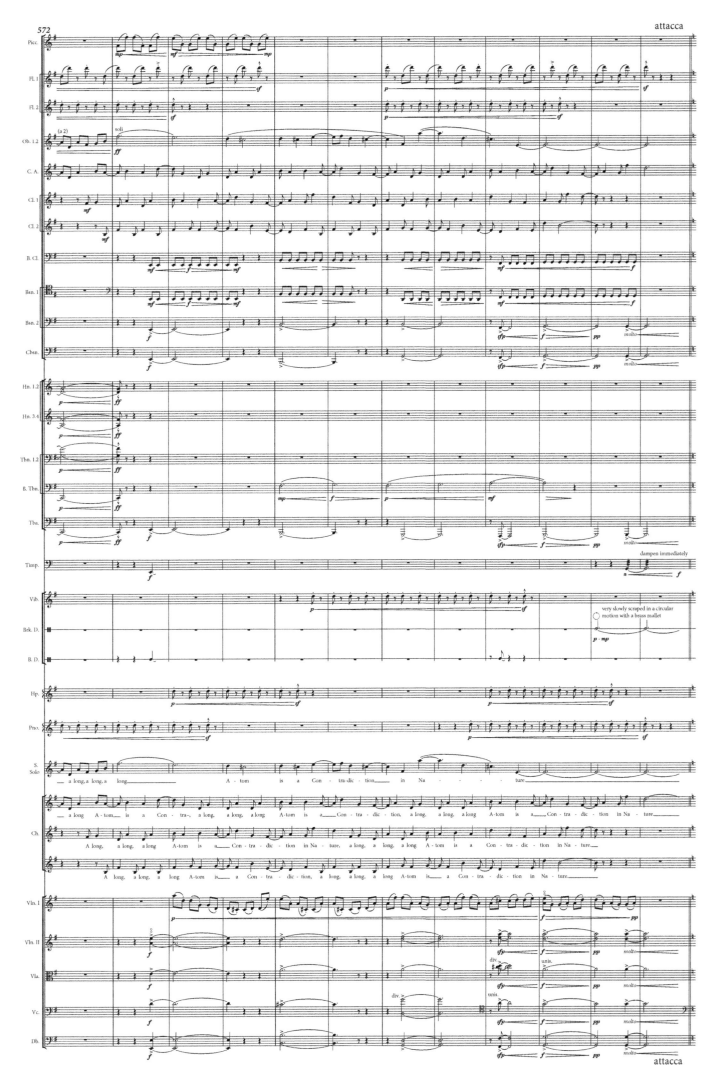

attacca

# 8. Night

*Man*
George Herbert

58

# 9. A Marvellous Body

*Centuries of Meditations*
Thomas Traherne

62

64